INCREDIBLY AWFUL JOKES

What does a comedian do when he's going out on his motorcycle?
He puts on a helmet and giggles!

Friend — "Why did you lose your job as a pilot?"
Ex-pilot — "My work went into a decline!"

Fisherman — "I've worked on the trawlers all my life, hauling up one net after another, day after day. . ."
Friend — "Life's a drag, isn't it!"

Friend — "So you gave up your job running the carousel?"
Fairground attendant — "Yes — things took a turn for the worse!"

Farmer — "My horse does impressions!"
Friend — "Really?"
Farmer — "Yes! He gave me an impression of his shoe on my backside!"

Rob — "Why did you lose your job as a dog-catcher, Bob?"
Bob — "Inflation!"
Rob — "Inflation?"
Bob — "Yes — I couldn't get many dogs to the pound any more!"

Friend — "So how's the window cleaning business going?"
Window cleaner — "It's a bit of a pane!"

Molly — "My sister works for an ironing service."
Maisie — "Does she earn much?"
Molly — "No, just a flat rate — but she's hoping for a pay in-crease soon!"

Why did the carpenter go to the doctor's?
Because he had a saw finger!

What happens when cows won't give milk?
The dairyman doesn't see the pint!

"What do you do for a living?"
"I sell salt!"
"Really? I'm a salt sellar too!"
"Shake!"

Friend — "Well, Gladys, how's your slimming club going?"
Gladys — "Very well! — for every pound my members lose, I gain two!"

1st man — "And what do you earn at the frozen foods factory?"
2nd man — "Ice lolly!"

How much do chicken farmers earn?
A poultry amount!

How did the ringmaster pay the strongman?
Weakly!

How did King Arthur pay the knights in his castle?
Fort-knightly!

What did the doctor say to his dog?
"Heal!"

Do anglers make any money?
Not much, but they sometimes get a couple of squid!

Why did the pianist refuse his salary cheque?
Because he wanted to be paid in notes!

Do hairdressers make a lot of money?
No — but there are plenty of fringe benefits!

Friend — "How is your new job as a lifeguard going?"
Lifeguard — "Oh, swimmingly, thanks!"

Farmhand to friend — "I used to have a job collecting eggs on a chicken farm, but I was laid off."

Friend — "Why on earth did you choose to be a rodeo rider?"
Rodeo rider — "I wanted lots of bucks!"

What do you call two lawyers in an underwear shop?
A pair of briefs!

What did the undertaker say when he knocked on the coffin lid?
"Is there any body in?"

Man to police officer — "Officer! Someone's dug an enormous hole in my front garden!"
Police officer — "We'll look into it right away, sir!"

Friend — "What's life like on the oil rigs?"
Oil rig worker — "Boring!"

Friend — "So you've given up Scottish country dancing — why is that?"
Dancer — "Problems, problems — it was just one fling after another!"

What does the detective carry to work with him?
An open-and-shut case!

Friend — "How exciting! Twin boys! Congratulations! How did the birth go?"
Musician — "Not bad at all of course, they arrived one sonata time!"

Friend — "How's the fireworks business?"
Fireworks manufacturer — "Business is booming!"

Friend — "How are you getting on in your new job as a bus driver?"
Bus driver — "Oh, not bad, but it's a bit stop-and-go!"

Friend — "So why did you give up your career as a sword swallower?"
Sword swallower — "I just couldn't see the point any more!"

Friend — "You're retiring from sprinting, are you? Why is that?"
Athlete — "I was getting too far behind!"

Friend — "Why did you give up swimming?"
Swimmer — "I threw in the towel!"

Friend — "So what are you going to do after you retire?"
Gardener — "Grow older!"

Friend — "Why did you give up your job on the farm?"
Farm worker — "It was the hay baling — that was just the last straw!"

Friend — "So you're retiring, are you? Why is that?"
Butcher — "I didn't retire — I was given the chop!"

Friend — "Why did you give up your job as a waiter?"
Waiter — "I had too much on my plate."

Dairyman to farmer — "I'm sick of this job! I'm going to look for an udder one!"

Friend — "Why did you give up your job as a tailor?"
Tailor — "The job didn't suit me!"

Friend — "Why did you leave the orchestra?"
Musician — "It all went rather flat!"

Friend — "So you've given up DIY — why is that?
DIY enthusiast — "I just didn't know what to do with my shelf any more!"

1st fisherman — "I hear you've got a great new job
— how did you find it?
2nd fisherman — "It was advertised on the Net!"

Why was the photographer depressed?
He kept seeing the negative side of things!

*Friend — "I hear you're giving up your job as a train driver
— what are you going to do next?"
Train driver — "I'll be looking for something else along the
same lines!"*

Did you hear about the absent-minded train-driver?
He lost track!

Why did the novelist go mad?
He lost the plot!

*Dry-cleaner to customer — "Sorry, madam, I can't
clean your curtains today. I have a pressing appointment
elsewhere!"*

Friend — "So you're giving up your dreams of being a
writer — what will you do next?"
Writer — "One chapter closes, another one opens. . ."

Friend — "Why did you give up your job in the duvet
factory?"
Duvet stuffer — "The job was getting me down."

Why did the sandwich-maker go to the dentist?
His fillings kept coming out!

Friend — "So you've given up your haggis-making business. Why is that?
Butcher — "I didn't have the guts for it any more!"

What did the architect's children say to him at bedtime?
"Give us another storey, Dad!"

Why did the theatre manager give up his job?
He wanted a change of scenery!

Why did the orange give up acting?
He didn't like the limelight!

Why did the miner give up his job?
It was the pits!

Why did the casino worker give up his job?
Someone offered him a better deal!

Will — "I was fired from my job, because they said I was slow at everything. But it's just not true!"
Bill — "Why not?"
Will — "Because I'm not slow at everything — I tire quickly!"

Friend — "What made you become an exorcist?"
Exorcist — "I don't know — I can't think what possessed me!"

Patient — "Can you recommend some cough mixture for me?"
Pharmacist — "This stuff's great — you won't get any better!"

Friend — "So you're not cutting grass any longer?"
Greenkeeper — "No — I'm cutting it shorter!"

Manager — "If you don't keep up with your work, I'm going to have to get another man!"
Worker — "Thank goodness! I could do with an assistant!"

Why is a tree surgeon like an actor?
Because he takes boughs!

Interior designer — "The room's nearly finished, but I think you should get a chandelier!"
Client — "What would be the point? No-one in our family plays one!"

Notice outside dry-cleaners "We'll clean for you, we'll press for you — we'll even dye for you!"
Instructor — "You're ready to fly solo today!"
Trainee pilot — "How low?"

Friend — "Why did you get a job at the bank?"
Bank clerk — "Because there's money in it!"

Will — "My brother's an exporter!"
Bill — "Does he send goods abroad?"
Will — "No — he used to work at the railway station!"

Book title — "Punctuality Pays" by Justin Time

Book title — "The Dangers of Coastal Cliffs" by Eileen Dover

Book title — "Success in the Christmas Sales" by Jocelyn Ann Grabbin

Book title — "The Key to Happiness" by Eve R. Smylie

Book title — "Fishing is Fun" by Rod N. Lyne

Book title — "1000 funny stories" by Owen Lee Joe King

Book title — "Writing a Bestseller" by Will U. Buyatt

Book title — "Laundry Tips" by Crispin White

Book title — "My life as a prize-fighter" by K.O.D. Best

Book title — "Archery for Beginners" by Pierce Stallover

Book title — "Notes from a Desert Island" by I. Malone

Book title — "Life on the Beach" by Sandy Shaw

Book title — "Living discreetly" by Annette Curtain

Book title — "Amazing ball tricks" by C. Lyon

Book title — "Successful partnerships" by Mary A. Richman

Book title — "How a Steamroller Changed My Life" by I.M. Flatman

Book title — "How to avoid sunburn" by C.U. Redden

Book title — "1000 Questions & Answers" by Noah Lotte

Book title — "My life as a lion tamer" by Claude B. Hind

Book title — "How to Get Rich" by Mary A. Tycoon

Book title — "Successful Orienteering" by Ivor Mappe

Book title — "Deep-sea Fishing for Women" by Netta Shark

Book title — "Gem-hunting" by Williamina Ruby

Holiday reading for gardeners "Ivanhoe"!

Holiday reading for welders anything riveting!

Holiday reading for furniture sales staff
"A Tale of Two Settees"!

Holiday reading for electricians
"The Vital Spark"!

Holiday reading for firefighters
The Complete Works of Burns!

Holiday reading for goat-keepers — "Kidnapped"!

Holiday reading for musicians — "Murder on the High C's"!

Holiday reading for genealogists — "Goldilocks and the Forebears"!

Holiday reading for magicians — "Tom Saw-yer"!

Holiday reading for indecisive people — "Maybe Dick"!
Holiday reading for mothers-to-be — "Great Expectations"!

Holiday reading for acrobats — some magazines to flip through!

Holiday reading for monsters — The Tales of Grimm

Holiday reading for hairdressers — "Tess of the Barbervilles"!

Holiday reading for knights — "David Coppershield"!

Holiday reading for bakers — anything by Agatha Crusty!

Holiday reading for dog-lovers — "The Beagle has Landed"!

Honeymoon reading for nits — "Brideshead Revisited"!

Holiday reading for florists —
"How to Twine Fronds and Influence People".

Holiday Reading for skiers —
"Slithering Heights"!

Holiday reading for ballroom dancers —
"The Thirty-nine Steps"!

Holiday reading for herbalists —
"A Brief History of Thyme"!

Holiday reading for grasshoppers —
"What Katydid"!

Holiday reading for fortune-tellers —
"The Foresight Saga"!

Reading for sleeping under the stars — "The Wind in the Pillows"!

Reading for orbiting astronauts —
"Around the World for Eighty Days"!

Why do surgeons wear gloves?
Because their patients are out cold!

What do an anaesthetist and a baked bean have in common?
They both give you gas!

Why did the surgeon x-ray his stomach?
He wanted to be on bellyvision!

Patient; — "Doctor, doctor, I'm all fingers and thumbs!"
Doctor — "In that case, can you lend me a hand?"

Patient — "Well, doctor, what do you think is wrong with me — measles or chickenpox?"
Doctor — "To be honest, I can't spot the difference!"

Patient — "Doctor, doctor, I've swallowed the ring I was going to give my wife!"
Doctor — "There's nothing I can do — but wrap up carefully for the present!"

Patient — "Doctor, doctor! I've been bitten by a dog!"
Doctor — "Name?"
Patient — "Rover!"

Nurse — "I drove into the hospital today!"
Patient — "Did you?"
Nurse — "So don't worry about the noise — they're just repairing the wall!"

Patient — "Doctor, doctor, I've swallowed a fly — should I take something for it?"
Doctor — "No — just let it starve!"

Patient — "Doctor, doctor! I feel like an aeroplane!"
Doctor — "Give me a wing tomorrow!"

Patient — "Doctor, doctor, everybody treats me like a cricket ball!"
Doctor — "How's that?"
Patient — "See what I mean?"

Doctor — "Drink plenty of fluids, and keep away from draughts!"
Patient — "I can't stand that game anyway!"

Patient — "Doctor, doctor, I'm locked out!"
Doctor — "That's no concern of mine!"
Patient — "Yes it is — my son's swallowed the key!"

Patient — "Doctor, doctor, I'm a terrible liar!"
Doctor — "I don't believe a word you're saying!"
Nurse — "Have you found the golf ball the patient swallowed?"
Surgeon — "Yes — here it is!"
Nurse — "Right, I'll call in the other man to take his next shot, then!"

Doctor — "This is a very strange problem, Mrs Green! Have you had it before?"
Mrs Green — "Yes, doctor!"
Doctor — "Well — you've got it again!"

Patient — "Doctor, doctor, can you recommend something for my liver?"
Doctor — "Onions, gravy and some creamed potatoes!"

Patient — "Doctor, doctor, I've put my back out!"
Doctor — "Shouldn't have done that — you need it to hold your neck up!"

Patient — "Doctor, doctor! I still feel like an aeroplane!"
Doctor — "Wait one moment please!"
Patient — "Sorry — can't stop — must fly!"

Patient — "Doctor, doctor, can you treat me?"
Doctor — "Certainly not! Pay at the desk as you go out!"

Patient — "Doctor, doctor, I think I'm a ladder!"
Doctor — "Have you rung me about this before?"

Patient — "I'm very nervous — this is my first operation!"
Surgeon — "That makes two of us!"

Nurse — "Doctor, doctor, what have you done to my book?"
Doctor — "Nothing to worry about, nurse — I just removed its appendix!"

Patient — ". . . and I think that's all, doctor!"
Doctor — "I certainly hope so! Now, excuse me one moment while I write out something for you!"
Patient — "A prescription?"
Doctor — "With all your complaints a prescription wouldn't do the trick at all. . .No, I'm writing you a letter of introduction to the undertaker!"

Patient — "Will you give me something for my legs, doctor?"
Doctor — "How about a decent pair of trousers?"

Patient — "Doctor, doctor, I've got an enormous pimple!"
Doctor — "That zit, is it?"

Patient — "Doctor, doctor, I've got a headache, my joints are painful and I'm running a fever!"
Doctor — "Flu?"
Patient — "No, I came by taxi!"

Doctor (calling at patient's house) —
"This is serious! Have you got a hammer and chisel?"
Patient — "You're not going to use them on me, are you doctor?"
Doctor — "No — I've locked myself out of my car again!"

What did the surgeon say to the patient on the operating table?
"Right — that's quite enough out of you!"

Doctor — "Well, Mr Smith, I've got good news and bad news!"
Mr Smith — "What's the bad news?"
Doctor — "You're seriously ill!"
Mr Smith — "And the good?"
Doctor — "I've won the surgery sweepstake!"

Patient — "Doctor, doctor, my last doctor thought I was a dog!"
Doctor — "Why do you say that?"
Patient — "Well, he told me I had a terrible bark and gave me some 'ruff' treatment!"

Patient — "Doctor! Doctor! I don't feel so hot!"
Doctor — No wonder! You have a cold!"

Patient — "Doctor, doctor, can I tell you something about this germ I've caught?"
Doctor — "No! No! You mustn't spread it around!"

Patient — "This dressing you've given me is playing a tune!"
Nurse — "Yes — it's a band-aid!"

Nurse — "Well, Mr Brown, you may have a broken leg, but with my help you can still jump over two men!"
Patient — "What do you mean?"
Nurse — "I've brought you a game of checkers!"

Doctor — "You are going to need an operation, but I'm afraid you'll have to wait for a hospital bed!"
Patient — "As long as it gets there before I come round, I don't mind!"

Doctor — "So you thought you were a werewolf, did you, Mr Jones?"
Patient — "Yes, Doctor, but I'm all right Now-oo-ooh!"

Patient — "Doctor, doctor, I've got insomnia!"
Doctor — "Never mind that — why are you late for your appointment?"
Patient — "I overslept!"

Patient — "Doctor, doctor, I fell down the stairs!"
Doctor — "And where did you hurt yourself?"
Patient — "From top to bottom!"

Doctor — "Don't worry, Mr Jones, the injection won't hurt a bit!"
Mr Jones — "OW! I thought you said it wouldn't hurt!"
Doctor — "It didn't — I hardly felt a thing!"

Doctor — "Nurse! What is your weedy boyfriend doing in my hospital?"
Nurse — "You told me to bring you a drip!"

Patient — "Doctor, Doctor, my mother thinks she's a goose!"
Doctor — "I'd better look at her at once!"
Patient — "You can't see her, I'm afraid — she's flown south for the winter!"

Patient — "Doctor, doctor, I'll lay odds of five to one that you don't know what's wrong with me!"
Doctor — "Ah, better already, I see!"

Witch — "Doctor, doctor, my friend here thinks she's invisible!"
Doctor — "NURSE! NURSE! There's a woman here who thinks she's got an invisible friend!"

Patient — "Doctor, doctor, I think I'm a horse!"
Doctor — "Take these pills to make you stable!"

Patient — "Doctor, doctor, I feel as if there's a great black cloud hanging over me!"
Doctor — "Don't worry, you're just under the weather!"

Patient — "Doctor, you must make me better — I'm taking part in the Olympics next week!"
Doctor — "Dear, oh, dear — you have a temperature of 105 degrees!"
Patient — "That's my personal best!"

Patient — "Doctor, doctor, I've got hives!"
Doctor — "Thought of taking up bee-keeping?"

Doctor — "I gave you a repeat prescription last week, Mrs Smith — how are you now?"
Mrs Smith — "I'm all right now, I'm all right now, I'm all right now, I'm all right now!"

Patient — "Doctor, doctor, I've drilled a hole in my finger!"
Doctor — "Which part?"
Patient — "This bit here!"

Doctor — "So you lose your temper every time someone calls you a name? Surely that can't be true!"
Patient — "DON'T CALL ME SHIRLEY!"

Patient — "Doctor, doctor, I think I'm a cat!"
Doctor — "Don't worry, Mr Jones, I'm an ex-purr-t!"

Patient — "Doctor, doctor, I think I'm an insect!"
Doctor — "Beetle off and fetch the next patient, will you?"

Patient — "Doctor, doctor, I feel really funny!"
Doctor — "Tell us a joke, then!"

Patient — "Doctor, doctor, I've got pins and needles!"
Doctor — "Here's material and some thread; — make me some new curtains for the waiting room!"

Doctor — "This is very serious! I'm calling an ambulance!"
Patient — "What is it, doctor?"
Doctor — "It's a van with a flashing blue light that will get you to hospital quickly!"

Patient — "Doctor, doctor, I've got carrots growing from my ears!"
Doctor — "I can't understand it!"
Patient — "Nor can I — I planted potatoes!"

Patient — "Doctor, doctor, I've got insomnia!"
Doctor — "Well, you mustn't lose any sleep over it!"

Patient — "Doctor, doctor, I think I'm changing into a fish!"
Doctor — "Oh, you poor sole!"

Patient — "Doctor, doctor, I feel like a caterpillar!"
Doctor — "You little creep!"

Patient — "Doctor, doctor, I think my wife is a ghost!"
Doctor — "Why do you say that?"
Patient — "Because she looks a fright!"

Patient — "Doctor, doctor, my wife thinks she's the Queen!"
Doctor — "And how does she feel?
Patient — "Grand!"

Patient — "Doctor, doctor, I keep hearing music in my head!"
Doctor — "Just one moment, while I read your notes..."

Patient — "Doctor, doctor, I've got my head stuck in this piece of luggage!"
Doctor — "Come into the surgery and I'll take a look at you — just in case!"

Doctor — "What seems to be the trouble, Mrs Smith?"
Mrs Smith — "You tell me — you're the doctor!"

Doctor — "I tell you, nurse, I've never lost a patient!"
Nurse — "But all your patients are dead and buried!"
Doctor — "Yes — and I know exactly where each one of them can be found!"

Patient — "Doctor, doctor, I make a mewing sound whenever I breathe through my nose!"
Doctor — "Nothing to worry about, Mr Brown; it's just cat-arrh!"

Patient — "Doctor, doctor, it's me bloomin' back again!"
Doctor — "Yes it's you, bloomin' back again — but what's the bloomin' matter?"

Patient — "Doctor, doctor, my shoulders keep jerking up and down. Is it serious?"
Doctor — "Don't worry — you'll soon shrug it off!"

Patient — "Doctor, doctor, I've just swallowed a roll of camera film!"
Doctor — "We'll have to wait a few days for developments."

Patient — "Doctor, doctor, I feel like a baby!"
Doctor — "Don't come crawling to me!"

Patient — "Doctor, doctor, I've become a terrible thief!"
Doctor — "You'll have to take something for that!"

Patient — "Doctor, doctor, look at all these insects buzzing about my head!"
Doctor — "Don't worry, there are a lot of bugs going round at this time of year!"

Patient — "Doctor, doctor, what did you see when you X-rayed my head?"
Doctor — "Absolutely nothing!"

Doctor — "Now, Mrs Jones, say Aaa-aah!"
Mrs Jones — "Aaa-aah!"
Doctor — "Oh, dear, oh dear! — Now, Mrs Jones, cough!. . . and again. . . and again. . . and again. . . and again. . ."
Mrs Jones — "For heaven's sake, doctor, whatever is the matter with me?"
Doctor — "Nothing — I dropped a contact lens down your throat, and I'm trying to get it back!"

Doctor — "Don't worry, Mrs Jones, I've been practising medicine for seventeen years?"
Mrs Jones — "If you've been practising for seventeen years, how come you still can't do it right?"

Patient — "Doctor, doctor, I think I'm a bear!"
Doctor — "And how long have you been feeling this way?"
Patient — "Ever since I was a cub!"

Patient — "Doctor, doctor, I was drinking tea last night when I suddenly got a terrible pain in my eye!"
Doctor — "You left the spoon in the mug again!"

Patient — "Doctor, doctor, my ears have dropped off!"
Doctor — "Let's face it, sir you're not all there any more!"

Patient — "Doctor, doctor, I swallowed a bone!"
Doctor — "You're choking!"
Patient — "No, honestly, I really did!"

Patient — "Doctor, doctor, can you give me something for wind?"
Doctor — "How about a kite?"

Patient — "Doctor, doctor, I think I'm a mountain!"
Doctor; — "Well, you do look peaky!"

Patient — "Doctor, doctor, my wife ironed my clothes while I was still wearing them!"
Doctor — "And how do you feel?"
Patient — "Rather flat!"

Doctor — "Back again, Mrs Smith? You were only here yesterday! What can I do for you?"
Mrs Smith — "I've come back for a second opinion!"

What did the doctor say when Dracula came to see him?
"Necks, please!"

Patient — "Doctor, doctor, I think I'm a pop star!"
Doctor — "Don't worry, you're getting on famously!"

Patient — "Doctor, doctor, my skin's turning gold!"
Doctor — "Looks like a gilt complex to me!"

Why did the banker go to the doctor's?
For a cheque-up!

Why is a doctor like a comedian?
They both have people in stitches!

Patient — "Doctor, doctor, I think I'm a snail!"
Doctor — "Don't worry, you'll soon come out of your shell!"

Patient — "Doctor, doctor, I took the medicine you gave me and I still feel like ten-pound note!
Doctor — "No change yet, then!"

Patient — "Doctor, doctor, I've got a stitch in my side!"
Doctor — "So what? I've got hundreds in my jumper!"

Mrs McTavish — "Well, ye see, doctor, I've got a wee cough..."
Doctor — "A whole week? I haven't even had a day off all year!"

Patient — "Doctor, doctor, I think I'm a moth!
Doctor — "But why did you come round here so late at night?"
Patient — "Well, I saw the light at your window. . ."

Mr and Mrs Bloggs — "Doctor, doctor, our new baby doesn't look like us at all!"
Doctor — "I know. Lucky little thing, isn't he?"

Patient — "Doctor, doctor, can you help me out, please?"
Doctor — "Certainly. The door's just over there!"

Patient — "Doctor, doctor, I think I'm a duck!"
Doctor — "You're quackers!"

Patient — "Doctor, doctor, what can you recommend for food poisoning?"
Doctor — "Well, eating half-cooked chicken might do it..."

Patient — "Doctor, doctor, I feel like a bridge!"
Doctor — "Like a bridge? What's come over you?"
Patient — "Two cars, a bus and a lorry so far. . ."

Patient — "Doctor, doctor, I've hurt my leg!"
Doctor — "Where does it hurt?"
Patient — "Everywhere I walk!"

Patient — "Doctor, doctor, I think I've got chickenpox!"
Doctor — "What are you complaining about? Every time I look at you I get spots before my eyes!"

Patient — "Doctor, doctor, I've got blurred vision!"
Doctor — "Have you tried cleaning your spectacles?"

Patient — "Doctor, doctor, I can't hear properly!"
Doctor — "Take your earmuffs off, Mrs Jones!"

Patient — "Doctor, doctor, I don't feel well!"
Doctor — "Take your mittens off, Mrs Green!"

Patient — "Doctor, doctor, I've got hot flushes!"
Doctor — "I told you that plumber was useless!"

Patient — "Doctor, doctor, my foot — it's just not right!"
Doctor — "That's because it's your left foot, Mr Brown!"

Patient — "Doctor, doctor, I've got a tight feeling round my chest!"
Doctor — "Your vest's too small, Mr Bloggs!"

Patient — "Doctor, doctor, I'm choking!"
Doctor — "No you're not — your scarf has caught on the door!"

Fred — "When's your birthday?"
Ted — "10th June!"
Fred — "What year?"
Ted — "Every year!"

Daisy — "Dad's spent all morning doing something impossible!"
Dora — "What's that?"
Daisy — "He's been looking round for a pencil behind his ear!"

How can you ask a blunt knife to do the impossible?
Tell it to look sharp!

What happened when the astronaut tried to read a book in zero gravity?
He couldn't put it down!

Sergeant — "How did the thief escape? I told you to cover all exits!"
P.C — "He got out the entrance, sir!"

Will — "Has your girlfriend gone off in a huff again?"
Bill — "No — she's taken the bus!"

What's black and white and noisy?
A zebra with a drum kit!

"Have you ever chased elephants on horseback?"
"Don't be silly — elephants don't ride horses!"

Mum — "Are you sweeping out the lounge, as I asked?"
Son; — "No — just the dust!"

Man (to singer) — "Can you sing 'Over the Hills and Far
Away?"
Singer — "Yes, I can!"
Man — "Well, off you go, then!"

Man — "Do you know 'Loch Lomond'?"
Singer — "Yes, I do!"
Man — "Well go and jump in it!"

"Are you hungry?"
"Yes, Siam!"
"Come on then, I'll Fiji!"

Man — "Is this river good for fish?"
Angler — "It must be — they refuse to come out!"

Two lorries crashed at a junction One was carrying
purple paint, the other red,
The drivers are marooned on the island in the middle of
the road!
Bill — "Dark, isn't it?"
Will — "Dunno — can't see to tell!"

Bill — "Am I handsome or ugly?"
Will — Both — you're pretty ugly!"

"Open Seasme!"
"Open says-a who?"

"I didn't come here to be insulted!"
"Where do you usually go?"

"A donkey wants to cross a river, but there's no bridge, no boat, the water's very deep and the donkey can't swim. What does he do?"
"I give up!"
"So did the donkey!"

Why did the teddy bears leave the building site today?
Because today's the day the teddy bears have their picks nicked!

"My girlfriend's one of twins!"
"How can you tell them apart?"
"Her brother has a beard!"

Fred — "my dog's really lazy — I was watering the garden and he wouldn't lift a leg to help me!"

"My bird can talk and it lays square eggs!"
"What does it say?"
"Ouch!"

Why did the mummy kangaroo have a sore tummy?
Because her baby was bouncing in bed!

What did the germ say to its friend?
"Keep away! I've got a dose of antibiotics!"

Where does Thursday come before Wednesday?
In a dictionary!

When is a car like a golfer?
When it goes 'Putt, putt, putt!"

Receptionist — "I'm sorry, but the doctor can't see you just now!"
Patient — "Why not?"
Receptionist — "Because he's in the other room, silly!"

When is a hat like an injection?
When it's felt!

Patient — "Doctor, doctor, I was walking barefoot in the park and I cut my foot!"
Doctor — "Must have been a sharp blade of grass!"

Patient — "Doctor, doctor, my ears keep ringing!"
Doctor — "Have your number changed!"

Patient — "Doctor, doctor, I've just been attacked by a giant ladybird!"
Doctor — "That'll be one of these superbugs they're always talking about!"

Lady in phone box — "Emergency services? A man has just been knocked down by a car outside his house!"
Operator — "Keep calm, and try to tell us how to get to you!"
Lady — "Haven't you got an ambulance or something?"

Will — "I was on the way to the doctor's and I met three women, two children and six men!"
Bill — "So how many people went to the doctor's with you?"
Will — "None! They were all coming back!"

Will — "My doctor carries a cat in the back of his car!"
Bill — "Really?"
Will — "Yes — it's the first-aid kit!"

Patient — "Doctor, doctor! My left side is crumbling away!"
Doctor — "Don't worry — you'll soon be all right!"

Patient — "Doctor, doctor, my sheets keep falling off the bed!"
Doctor — "Don't worry, the nurses will help with your recovery!"

Doctor — "Well, Mr Smith, I've got good news and bad news!"
Hospital patient — "What's the good news?"
Doctor — "We're sending you home today!"
Patient — "And the bad?"
Doctor — "Your house burned down last night!"

Three crows sitting on the wall. A man shoots one.
How many are left?
None — the others fly away!

What colour is a hiccup?
Burple!

A family of tortoises are eating in a café. Baby tortoise is sent to wash his hands before they have their ice cream. The ice cream arrives and the baby tortoise still isn't back.
"Perhaps we'd better eat his ice cream, before it melts," says Mummy.
"If you do that," says a voice from the edge of the room, "I won't even go!"

What do men do standing, ladies do sitting, and dogs do on three legs?
Shake hands!

"Is that your black dog?"
"No — I've got a greyhound!"

What is the shortest job?
An astronaut — they are hired — then they're fired!

Did you hear about the unfortunate archeologist?
He got buried in his work!

What is the name of the woman in charge of the space programme?
Kate Canaveral!

What is open when it's shut and shut when it's open?
A level crossing!

What happens if you swallow uranium?
You get atomic-ache!

What do you get if you cross chocolate with a sheep?
A Hershey Baa-aa!

What's yellow and dangerous?
A herd of thundering bananas!

What are nitrates?
More expensive than day rates!

Have you heard the joke about the rope?
Oh — skip it!

Customer — "But you said my car was rust-free!"
Car salesman — "Exactly — we don't charge a penny for the rust!"

Bill — "What do you think of monogamy?"
Will — "It's not bad — but I prefer pine!"

How do you make a lamb stew?
Keep it waiting!

Why was Humpty-Dumpty a disappointment?
He wasn't All he was cracked up to be!

Don't swim in the river in Paris —
It's in Seine!

Butcher — "I've got liver, kidneys, heart. . ."
Customer — "I came here for meat — not an organ recital!"

Bill — My friend's so mean that he bought a house with tiny rooms so that he could use smaller lightbulbs!
Will — My friend's so mean that he goes visiting whenever it gets dark, so he doesn't have to use lightbulbs at all!

Fred — My friend's always exaggerating — he told me he was rolling in dough, but he hardly has two pennies to rub together!
Ted — My friend told me he was rolling in dough as well — when he got a job at the bakery!

Why was the butcher a bully?
Because he made mincemeat of the steak!

Little boy — *"Why do bulls wear rings through their noses?"*
Dad — *"Because they don't have fingers, son!"*

What do hitch-hikers carry for emergencies?
A truck-sack!

Why did the hitch-hiker stay at home?
Because he felt like doing thumb-thing different for a change!

Maisie — *"That hitch-hiker looks familiar!"*
Mo — *"That's because we've seen him at least five times before!"*
Maisie — *"How's that?"*
Mo — *"Because you're driving round in circles!"*

Why did the criminal drive past the prison?
He was taking the see-nick route home!

Minister — *"Envy is a sin — you must not be jealous of other people's possessions."*
Burglar — *"Oh, I never do that!"*
Minister — *"Really?"*
Burglar — *"No! I'm never envious of other people's possessions — I just take them!"*

Mum — "George! I keep telling you not to be greedy, but you're eating enough for two!"
George — "It's not because I'm greedy, Mum — it's because I'm twice as hungry as anyone else!"

Mum — "Billy? Did you break the window?"
Billy — "Well, Mum, I would be lying if I said I didn't, but I would be a fool if I said that I did!"

Mum — *"What race are you taking part in on Sports Day, Jimmy?"*
Jimmy — *"The race to the ice-cream tent!"*

Little boy — "Help! Help! I can't swim!"
Lazy Lifeguard — "Stand up! Stand up! You're in the shallow end!"

Teacher — "Does anyone know what eidelweiss is?"
Pupil — "It's a vice, miss — there's greed, there's envy, and then there's sloth — the eidelweiss!"

Boastful — *"I lost my aeroplane in the Bermuda Triangle!"*

Forgetful — "I lost my car in Trafalgar Square!"
Cheerful — "I lost my bike, but it's somewhere a-round!"

Boastful — "I left my old life far behind me."
Romantic — "I left my heart in San Francisco."
Surprised — "I left my socks on in bed last night!"

Achiever — "I've come a long way to get where I am!"
Traveller — "I've come far from my roots to settle in
this place!"
Sponger — "I've come from next door to borrow some
milk!

Why did the library book cry?
Because it didn't like being a-loan!

What is small, blue, and eats mud?
A small blue mud-eater!

Nasty Nora — "Are you in a hurry?"
Nice Nancy — "No — why?"
Nasty Nora — "Because your make-up's been running all the
way here!"

What did the parking attendant say to his friend?
"Wanna come and play on my pay-station?"

Rude Ron — "You've got a Roman nose!"
Polite Pete — "Have I?"
Rude Ron — "Yes — it's roamin' all over your face!"

Bill — "Do you know the sun burns?
Will — "No — but I could sing you a couple of verses of
'Moon River'!"

Fred — "How did you learn that quicksand was dangerous?"
Ted — Oh — it didn't take long to sink in!"

Maisie — "Mo — your eyes look awfully far apart today — what's wrong with them?"
Maisie — "Nothing — my plaits are too tight, that's all!"

Man in chemist's shop — "Why are you tip-toeing?"
Pharmacist — "I'm trying not to wake the sleeping pills!"

Why is Europe like a frying pan?
Because it has Greece at the bottom!

Mr Dopey — "There's something wrong with this television — it will only show a picture of a revolving potato!"
Repair man — "That's not the television — that's your lunch in the microwave!"

Molly — "Will you join me in a pot of tea?"
Mo — "Not likely! The water's far too hot in there!"

What did the alien say to the petrol pump?
"Don't pick your nose while I'm talking to you!"

Bill — "I was riding the rollercoaster at the fair the other day, and my watch slipped off my wrist!"
Will — "Time flies when you're enjoying yourself!"
Bill — "Your sister certainly likes peanuts!"
Will — "Yes — elephants usually do!"

Will — "I'm in love with Mrs Mopp, the cleaner!"
Bill — "Did she sweep you off your feet, then?"

Will — "I'm in love with Miss Briggs, the optician!"
Bill — "Was it love at short sight, then?"

Will — "Where might you find dandruff?"
Bill — "Ask Mrs Druff — she might know where he is!"

How can you recognise Mr Dopey at the car wash?
He's the one on the motorbike!

Bill — "Why have you got a bandage on your ear?"
Will — "I burnt it!"
Bill — "How?"
Will — "Someone phoned me while I was doing the ironing!"

What's the difference between leather and bananas?
Leather makes shoes, but bananas make slippers!

Did you hear the joke about time?
It's not worth telling!

What has ten feet and sings?
A quintet!

Man passing chip shop with friend — "What's that terrible smell?"
Friend — "That's the UFO's!"
Man — "UFO's?"
Friend — "Unidentified Frying Objects!"

What do you get if you take a hand-held vacuum cleaner out on a windy day?
A dust-guster!

Why did Mr Dopey iron his face?
Someone told him he had wrinkles!

Did you hear about the soldier who got a job in the cookhouse?
The chef asked him to shell the eggs and he blew the kitchen wall down!
How can you recognise a worried farmer?
His eyebrows are furrowed!

Fred — "Do you know any animals that are peculiar to Great Britain?"
Ted — "A duck-billed platypus!"
Fred — "But there are no duck-billed platypuses in Great Britain!"
Ted — "And that's what makes it peculiar!"

1st man — "Why are you carrying that chest of drawers along the street?"
2nd man — "Because it refuses to walk!"

Bill — "I just saw a bus driver go straight past the traffic lights and into a shop!"
Will — "And what happened next?"
Bill — "He bought a newspaper, came out, and went back to where he had parked the bus!

Mum — "What's that noise in the kitchen?"
Son — "I'm just clearing away the dishes! — Where are the brush and shovel kept?"

Why was the bridesmaid arrested?
Because she held up a train!

Bill — "My, this fog is thick! I can't see my hands in front of my face!"
Will — "That's because they're in your pockets!"

Did you hear about the dopey man who wanted to start a chicken farm?
He went out and bought fifty eggplants!

Ike — "My car was run into by a lorry yesterday — you have no idea what I went through!"
Mike — "From the look of you I can guess — it was the windscreen!"

Man in boat — "Here — take my hand! The current's too strong for swimming!"

Man in water — "I'm not swimming — I'm riding my bike!"

Bill — "I keep racing pigeons!"
Will — "And if you keep racing them long enough, you might win!"

Major — "Who's that, playing the 'Last Post' so badly?"
Sergeant — "Corporal Jones, sir — we call him the Lone Bungler!"

Man to friend — "I need your advice. My son's just told me he wants to be a racing driver!"
Friend — "Whatever you do, don't stand in his way!"

Did you hear about the lighthouse keeper's accident?
He ran up the spiral staircase so fast that he screwed himself into the roof!

Save money — take up boxing and live on scraps!

Did you hear about the butler who raced his lordship?
He took the silver!

"Romeo — Romeo! Wherefore art thou, Romeo?"
Romeo appears from the bushes and stares up at his
sweetheart on the balcony.
"I've made you some dinner, Romeo," she calls, "A nice
piece of steak!"
"Yummy!" says Romeo, and catches the tasty morsel that is
thrown down to him. He tries to take a bite. It's rather tough,
but he sets to work with his strong white teeth. . .
Some years later, a young man called Will sits down at his
desk with his pen. Carefully, he writes out the title of his new
play: "Romeo Ain't Chewed it Yet"!

Sherlock — "I can tell you're wearing your winter underwear, Watson!"
Watson — "Incredible, Holmes! How did you deduce that?"
Sherlock — "Because you've forgotten to put your trousers on!"

First aid instructor — "Now, let's suppose someone picked up a very hot pan without wearing oven gloves, and burnt their hands. What would you do?"
Pupil — "Tell them to drop the pan, double-quick!"

Why was the prisoner's wife not allowed to see him on visiting day?
Because she had a ladder in her stocking!

Prison warder — "Why do you never get any letters from your friends, Wiggins?"
Prisoner — "Because they're all in here too!"

Lady (to charity collector on doorstep) — "No, I'm sorry, but I never give money to people at the door."
Charity collector — "Shall I knock at the window, then?"

Owner of country hotel — "We used to be haunted by a ghost who kept walking up and down the stairs all night. But things are a lot quieter since we had the place modernised!"
Visitor — "Why? Has he gone"
Owner — "No — he uses the lift!"

Two dogs are sitting watching the washing going round in the washing machine.
"What's on?" asks one.
"Soap!" says the other.

Railway station announcement — "The train on platform four will be back on the rails as soon as possible."!

Ted — "People who gamble are foolish!"
Fred — "But I don't gamble!"
Ted — "Then you're no better!"

Why are cameramen dangerous in the cinema?
Because they shoot films!

Driving instructor — "Right, Mrs Jones, release your clutch!"— so Mrs Jones let go of the steering wheel!

Fred — "My body is like a temple!"
Ted — "I know — an ancient ruin!"

A writer was very short of money, so he sent a letter to his friend, asking for a loan.
"I am penniless and I hope you will be kind enough to help me out," he wrote, "for I can't write on an empty stomach!"
His friend wrote back — "Indeed, you can't write on an empty stomach. Please find enclosed a pad of notepaper."

Absent-minded professor — "Don't I know you? Aren't you Mr Jones?"
Man — "No — I'm Mr Jones' twin brother!"
Absent-minded professor — "And the name is. . .?"

Fred — "How did you get that puncture, Ted?"
Ted — "I drove over a milk bottle!"
Fred — "What was a milk bottle doing in the middle of the road?"
Ted — "The milkman was carrying it!"

Bill — "Go straight along this road and you'll come to a sign for the village. You can't miss it!"
Five minutes later. . . "CRUMP!"
Will — "You were right!"

A businessman travelling from King's Cross to Waterloo settled himself on his seat in the train, dumped his briefcase beside him and went to sleep.
After a while he woke up, and realised the train was not moving.
"Are we in the station?" he asked the guard sleepily.
"Yes," said the guard.
So the businessman got off the train and the train moved away.
It was only then that he realised he was still in King's Cross!

Mum — "And what did the coach say when you scored a goal, son?"
Son — "He said next time I was to get it into the other team's net!"

Farmer — "My cow's grown a lot!"
Friend — "And I thought all cows went 'moo'!"

Explorer — "I've travelled all over South America!"
Bob — "So what? My goldfish travels round the globe several times a day!"

Ship's captain — "My, my, a singing whale! How do you think that has happened?"
Sailor — "I dropped my portable CD player overboard, sir!"

Stunt Pilot — "Looping-the-loop takes a lot of courage and skill, you know!"

Little boy — "Well, my granny taught me how to loop-the-loop when I was five, and it wasn't so bad!"

Stunt Pilot — "What do you mean by that?"

Little boy — "The knitting needles weren't nearly as sharp as I expected!"

Mail man — "Is this letter for you? The name on the envelope is smudged!"

Man — "Can't be for me, then — my name's Smith!"

Will — "It's quite possible to live on vegetables alone!"
Bill — "But it must get a little soggy underfoot when they go rotten!"

What is the latest letter in the alphabet?
'Y' — because it comes at the end of day!

Bill — "I just met a tall man with a black beard who said he went to school with you!"
Will — "There was no-one with a beard in my class at school!"

Burglar to accomplice — "I hear sirens — quick! Jump out of the window!"
Accomplice — "But we're on the thirteenth floor!"
Burglar — "Look, this is no time to be superstitious!"

Referee at football match — "Now, I want to see fair play and good sportsmanship in this match!"
Ape-like centre-forward — "Any more last wishes?"

How did the jester get promoted to royal puppeteer?
He pulled a few strings!

Maisie — "Have you noticed that ignorant people are often the loudest talkers?"
Mo — "Yes — and you don't have to shout!"

When is elastic like a microwave?
When it goes 'ping'!

Mr Dopey went ice-fishing
He caught twenty-five tons of ice!

Schoolboy's essay — "The Lone Ranger needed help fast, so he called for his friend Pronto!"

Two burglars are looting the home of a very wealthy tycoon. One of them is about to stand on a chair to reach a painting hanging on the wall. "Take your filthy shoes off first!" says his accomplice. "Have some respect for other people's property!"

Will — "Quite a small place, isn't it?"
Bill — "Yes — I had to remove the wallpaper to get the furniture in!"

A plane crashes on the border between France and Spain. Where are the survivors buried?
Nowhere! The survivors were still alive!

What happened to the shy stone?
It grew to become a little boulder!

Johnny — "I'm going out, Mum!"
Mum — "With that dirty face?"
Johnny — "No — with Bobby next door!"

Bill — "I once knew a man with very long arms. When he went up steps, he trod on them!"
Will — "His arms?"
Bill — "No — the steps!"

Why did the woman jump overboard?
Because the captain invited her to launch!

Ted — Which is right — nine and five is thirteen or nine and five are thirteen?"
Fred — "Neither — nine and five are fourteen!"

Maisie — "What is a buttress?"
Mo — "A female goat!"

Betty — "What is a water otter?"
Kitty — "A kettle!"

If it takes ten men three hours to dig a hole, how long does it take five men to dig half a hole?
They can't — there's no such thing as half a hole!

Billy — "Mum's given us two apples to share, but one's much bigger than the other!"
Bobby — "Do I get the choice?"
Billy — "Yes — you choose the smaller one or nothing!"

Two old men are sitting on a bench outside the old folk's home. The weather is breezy.
1st man — "Windy!"
2nd man — "Same here — must have been the beans!"

If you get hiccups, hold your breath for thirty seconds and they might go away.
— If that doesn't work, hold your breath for three hundred and thirty seconds, and you will never be troubled by hiccups again!

Later that same day. . .
1st man — "Still windy!"
2nd man — "No-Thursday!"
1st man — "Let's go for a drink then!"

Bill — "I'm exhausted!"
Will — "Why?"
Bill — "I hurt my leg and the doctor said I wasn't to climb the stairs for a week — you have no idea how difficult it is getting up the drainpipe every night!"

What did the robber call his horse?
Black Booty!

Billy — *"There was a hold-up at the bank yesterday!"*
bobby — *"So what? There was a hold-up in our garden today!"*
Billy — *"Really?"*
Bobby — *"Yes — ten pegs held up five shirts on the washing-line!"*

A policeman noticed a little girl with a suitcase trudging along the road. He was concerned to see a small child setting out on a journey all on her own, so he followed her to make sure she got to her destination safely. He followed her round one corner, round another corner and round another corner, and realised that they were now back where they started. He stopped the little girl and asked her what she was doing.
"I'm running away from home," she said.
"But all you are doing is walking round the block!" said the policeman.
"I know, said the little girl. "But I'm not allowed to cross the road!"

Burglar's son — "Dad, may I leave the table?"
Father — "Certainly not! We'll take it in the van with the rest of the loot!"

Owner of country mansion — "In the blue bedroom, you will see a plaque on the wall, telling you that Nelson once slept there!"
Visitor — "Why did he not use the bed?"

What word can no-one spell?
I'm sorry — I can't write it down — as I said, no-one can spell it!

What word is always spelt badly?
Badly!

Did you hear about the new superhero who cleans up after dogs? They've called him Scooperman!

Why is a ship's rudder like a policeman?
Because it has a stern duty to perform!

What is the sneakiest way to catch fish?
Swallow some worms, then wait by the side of the river with baited breath!

Helicopter passenger — "Pilot, it's rather cold up here! Do you think you could switch that fan off above our heads?"

What's the definition of a pyromaniac?
Someone with burning ambition!

Percy, the would-be pop star, rubbed the lamp in his dressing room one night, and a genie appeared.
"What is your desire, sir?" asked the genie.
Percy did not hesitate. "I would like to be surrounded by clamouring babes!" he said.
The next thing he knew, he was in the middle of the nursery in the maternity hospital!

What is the difference between a forged five-dollar note and an angry rabbit?
One is bad money, the other is a mad bunny!

Why did King Kong climb the Empire State Building?
He wanted to catch a plane!

"What does it feel like when you're half-way down the chimney, Santa?"
"Claus-trophobic!"

Tuneless singer — "I have to take care of my throat, doing what I do!"
Friend — "I expect you do, with all those people out there longing to throttle you!"

What do Nellie the Elephant and Alexander the Great have in common?
Their middle name!

Dad — "Come on, Shirley, get on with your homework. Homework never killed anyone yet!"
Shirley — "And I don't want to be the first to die!"

"I've bought a new hammer!"
"Watch out for the nail!"
"What nail?"
"The one on the end of your thumb!"

Will — "Do you realise that every time I breathe out, a person dies?"
Bill — "You should think about using mouthwash, then!"

Little boy — "I'd like a pound of bird seed for my cat, please!"
Pet-shop owner — "Why do you want bird-seed for your cat?"
Little boy — "how else am I going to feed the canary he swallowed?"

Little girl — "I don't know what to do with myself!"
Old Lady — "Why not?"
Little girl — "I've just found out that I'm the sort of child my mother doesn't want me to play with!"

Will — "What is the longest word you can think of?"
Bill — "Eternity!"

Father — "I taught my son everything I know!"
Friend — "He'll be ready for junior school soon, then!"

Zookeeper to young zoo visitor — "Have you come to see my long-eared antelope?"
Visitor — "Who is your long-eared aunt going to elope with?

Old Lady — "What do you want to be when you grow up, young man?"
Little boy — "I'd like to follow in my father's footsteps, ma'am!"
Old Lady — "So you want to be a doctor, too?"
Little boy — "No — I'll be the undertaker!"

Practise DIY in safety — get someone else to hold the nails while you hammer them!

Can you think of a container which has no lid, and which contains a golden secret?
An egg!

Bill — "Do you think it might rain today?"
Fred — "It depends on the weather!"

What is green, hairy and goes 'clickety-click?'
A ball-point gooseberry!

Why did the bald man stick his head out of the window?
He needed some fresh 'air!

The sheriff spent three weeks riding in the desert, looking for the rustlers. Finally, he had to admit defeat. He turned his horse around and headed back into town. Four days later, he rode into Dodge city. What did he say to his horse when he got back?
"Whoah!"

If a gallon of milk had a race with a litre of milk, which one would win?
The gallon would get the pints!

What's the difference between a needlewoman and a horse doctor?
One mends tears and the other tends mares!

What's black and white and bounces?
A zebra on a trampoline!
Anything else?
A nun on a pogo stick!
Anything else?
A rubber penguin

Molly — "My car is just like a baby"
Mo — "Why?"
Molly — "It never goes anywhere without a rattle!"

Bill — "Will, Will, we've got a gas leak in here!"
Will — "Don't panic — just put a bucket under it!"

What's the most popular place in town?
The cemetery — people are dying to get there!

Vet — "That's it, Mr Brown — your dog won't chase cars any more. I've cured him!"
Mr Brown — "How did you do that?"
Vet — "I tied his back legs together!"

What is the difference between a big black cloud and a child with toothache?
One pours with rain and the other roars with pain!

Have you heard the joke about the Eiffel Tower?
I don't think it's up your street!

Bill — "I'm selling my carpet. It's in mint condition!"
Will — "Yes — it's got a hole in the middle of it!"

Fred — "Your dog has been chasing me on my bike!"
Ted — "When did he learn to ride it?"

Who wears the biggest hat in the American navy?
The sailor with the biggest head!

Why did the dragon divorce his wife?
She kept smoking in bed!

Bill — "My dog's really stupid!"
Will — "What makes you say that?"
Bill — "He spent all afternoon chewing a bone, and
when he got up, he only had three legs!"

Teacher — "Half an hour ago, I caught you eating
chocolate, and now you're chewing gum! What
explanation have you got to offer for it?"
Pupil — "I finished all the chocolate!"

Teacher — "Tomorrow, we're going to the art gallery to
see some Old Masters."
Pupil — "Why? We've got plenty of them here!"

Pupil — "I've just discovered the hardest piece of
furniture in the world!"
Teacher — "And what is that?"
Pupil — "The multiplication table!"

Why did the scientist clone the trifle?
He wanted second helpings!

How can you hide in the desert?
Use camelflage!

Maisie — "My husband's in hospital. He was cutting down a tree in the garden the other day, when the chainsaw slipped and he cut off his leg!"
Annie — "Goodness. What did you do?"
Maisie — "I found someone else to cut the tree down!"

"I'm a little boy now, but when I was born, I was a little bare!"

What happened when the scientist cloned his girlfriend?
He fell in love with her all over again!

Did you hear about the man who wrote a poem first thing every morning, as soon as he got up?
He went from bed to verse!

What do you get if you cross a toaster with a hand-held vacuum cleaner?
A dust-cruster!

What happens if you put a brush in the fridge?
You get a br-rr-oom!

Friend — "How are you getting on writing your book?"
Writer — "I've written the end!"
Friend — "So you've finished?"
Writer — "No — I've written 'the end', and now I'm trying to think up the rest of the story!"

Did you hear about the egg in the monastery?
It went out of the frying pan into the friar!

What do you need if your toaster breaks down?
You need the bread to pop out for a new one!

Will — "My hamster got stuck in the tumble drier, and his name changed!"
Bill — "What do you mean?"
Will — "He went in Silky and he came out Fluffy!"

Lord and Lady Muck were holding a grand ball and they asked their chef to prepare some canapés to serve to their guests when they arrived. The great day dawned and Lord and Lady Muck went round the castle, checking that the servants had everything ready for the big night. Last of all they went into the kitchen, and found, to their surprise, that the cook was busily emptying packets of chewing gum into an enormous pan of hot oil.

"What are you doing? Have you gone mad?" screamed Lady Muck.

"No, ma'am," answered the cook. "I'm just making a little something for the guests. Haven't you heard the old saying? 'FRIED GUMS BEFORE A BALL'!"

Will — "Why are you covered in bruises, Bill?
Bill — "A ladder took a dislike to me!"
Will — "What do you mean by that?"
Bill — "It couldn't bear me!"

Will — "Why are you black and blue, Bill?"
Bill — "I was hit by a balloon!"
Will — "How could a balloon do so much damage?"
Bill — "It was stuck on the bonnet of a ten-ton truck!"

Mo (outside cemetery) — "I wouldn't like to be buried there!"
Maisie — "Why not?
Mo — "Because I'm still alive!"

Sailor — "There's something wrong with the boat, captain!"
Captain — "We'll have to take it to the dock!"

What day does the landlord collect the rent?
Duesday!

Dentist — "Looks like your lucky day!"
Golfer — "Why?"
Dentist — "You've got a hole in one!"

Did you hear about the criminal who took up German sausage-making?
He went from bad to wurst!

Where do Americans get their laundry done?
Washington!

Joe — "Can I stay over with Jimmy tonight, Mum?"
Mum — "But you don't have a sleeping bag!"
Joe — "It's all right — I'll take my knapsack!"

Teacher — "If I say the sentence 'I am beautiful', what tense am I using?
Pupil — "Pre-tense, miss!"

Billy — "Our teacher talks to herself!"
Bobby — "So does ours—but she thinks we're listening!"

Annie was late for school yesterday.
"Don't you dare walk into my classroom late again!" said the teacher.
So Annie didn't walk in late today.
She came in on rollerblades!

Pupil (at violin lesson) — "What would you like me to play?"
Music teacher — "Truant!"

Why did the sheikh not let his brother meet his wives?
He wanted to keep him out of harem's way!

What happened to the maths teacher in the jungle?
He added four and four, and got ate!

Did you hear about the vain nomad?
He spent too much time gazing into the mirage!

Did you hear about the latest invention to see through
the thickest of walls?
It's called a window!

Little girl — "I know a man who can go out in the rain
without getting his hair wet!"
Friend — "Who's that?"
Little girl — "My Dad — he's bald!"

When is a window like a star?
When it's a skylight!

Did you hear about the mad astronaut?
He went into space in a loony module!

What stays hot in the refrigerator?
Chilli!

"I was once glad to be down-and out!"
"When was that?"
"After a really bumpy plane ride!"

Why is honey scarce in Boston?
Because there's only one 'B' in Boston!

Did you hear about the wooden car?
It wooden go!

What did the balloon say to the pin?
"Hi, Buster!"

Why is a pair of handcuffs like a guide book?
Because it's for two-wrists!

Why is the letter 'D' like a naughty boy?
Because it makes ma mad!

What did the envelope say to the stamp?
"Stick with me, and you'll go places!"

Why was the tin of beans happy?
Because it was A-merry-can!

Did you hear about the smallest sailor?
He fell asleep on his watch!

"What's five Q and five Q?"
"Ten Q!"
"You're welcome!"

What's round and dangerous?
A vicious circle.

Annie — "What's the difference between a packet of cookies and a packet of fertilizer?"
Al — "I don't know!"
Annie — "I'm not coming round to your house for a snack, then!"

What colours should you paint the sun and the wind?
The sun rose, and the wind blew!

Ted — "My wife's gone on holiday to the West Indies!"
Fred — "Jamaica?"
Ted — "Certainly not — but I gave her plenty of encouragement!"

Where can you find letters that are not in the alphabet?
In a letterbox!

What walks on its head all day long?
A tack in your shoe!

Bill — "I'm glad you called me Bill!"
Bill's mum — "Why?"
Bill; — "Because that's my name!"

What do you call a couple of french fries, flying past each other in the darkness?
Chips that pass in the night!

What's the hardest thing about learning to ride a bike?
The ground!

What kind of bus crossed the ocean?
Columbus!

Why did the old man put wheels on his rocking chair?
To rock n' roll!

A man is standing at a bus stop, eating a hot dog. Beside him is a lady with a dog, and the dog is whining at the man. The man turns to the lady and says, "Do you mind if I throw him a bit?" and the lady says, "That would be very kind of you!"
So the man picks up the dog and throws him over the wall behind them!

"Which one of your sisters plays the mouth organ?"
"Oh — that'll be our Monica!"

"I've just seen two kangaroos tickling each other!"
"Don't be silly — it's just a hop-tockle illusion!"

Will — "Do you have any distant relatives?"
Bill — "No — they all live nearby!"

Bill — "I can tell you're enjoying your hot-dog!"
Will — "Really — how?"
Bill — "Because you're eating it with relish!"

Will — "Old George is really mean!"
Bill; — "How mean?"
Will — "So mean that when he pays you a compliment, he asks for a receipt!"

Coach — "Your career as football player is like a plane parked on the runway!"
Football player — "You mean it's ready to take off?"
Coach — "No — it's going nowhere!"

If two's company and three's a crowd, what are one and four?
Five!

Will — "Why are you going barefoot, Bill?"
Bill — "Because the road wears my shoes out!"

Mo — "I went out without my umbrella last night!"
Molly — "You must have got very wet!"
Mo — "No — it wasn't raining!"

What did the trousers say to the very short belt?
"Don't get around much, do you?"

Park-keeper — "Why have you stopped your car on the grass, sir? Don't you know it isn't allowed?"
Driver — "Why not? The sign says 'Park'!"

Maisie — "I met my first boyfriend in a revolving door!"
Mo — "Really?"
Maisie — "Yes — we went around together for ages!"

Politician's wife — "How did the crowd like your election speech?"

Politician — "Terrible — they threw eggs, tomatoes and potatoes at me!"

Politician's wife — "They really made a meal of you, didn't they!"

Mum — "A penny for your thoughts, Billy!"

Billy — "Have you never heard of inflation?"

What has three heads and three tails?
Three coins!

When is a car like a piece of music?
When it has four flats!

Bill — "Where are you going, Will?"
Will — "I'm going out to water the flowers!"
Bill — "But it's raining!"
Will — "That's all right — I'll take my umbrella!"

Jack — "My dog's like a grandfather clock!"
Mack — "Why's that?"
Jack — "Because he has a round face and ticks!"

Len — "My brother didn't say a word until he was five years old!"
Larry — "Then what happened?"
Len — "He picked up a wheel and spoke!"
Molly — "I fancy a great big doughnut!"
Mo — "You never had good taste in boyfriends!"

Annie — "Mum, what's the difference between a matador and a matadeer?"
Mum — "What's a matadeer?"
Annie — "Nothing! What's the matter with you?"

Jill — "What happened to your nose?"
Joe — "I hurt it smelling a brose!"
Jill — "There's no B in rose!"
Joe — "There was in this one!"

President — "Jackson! You can be my right-hand man!"
Jackson — "Sorry, Mr President, but I'm left handed!"

Traveller — "I've seen some spectacles in my time!"
Optician — "Not as many as I have, I'll bet!"

How do robots make their cars go faster?
They put the metal to the pedal!

Bill — "I wrote a letter to myself today!"
Will — "What did it say?"
Bill — "I don't know — it hasn't arrived yet!"

Monkey in safari park, watching visiting cars — "Look, they've brought more humans round to see us!"
Lion — "I know — but don't you think it's cruel keeping them caged up like that?"

Did you hear about the man who slept in just his underpants? He had a vestless night!

Maisie — "I put on lots of cream last thing every night!"
Mo — "So why are you covered in lumps and bumps?"
Maisie — "I keep slipping out of bed!"

Bill — "Your cooking's terrible!"
Mo — "How do you know?"
Bill — "A little bird told me!"
Mo — "What little bird?"
Bill — "A swallow!"

Farmer — "I've only got Fresian cows on my farm!"
Friend — "Why don't you ask your wife to knit you a Jersey?"

Fisherman (to fish) "I'm taking you home for dinner!"
Fish — "I've already had dinner — can we go to the movies instead?"

Bill; — "I can do the impossible!"
Will; — "What's that?"
Bill — "I can walk a mile and only move two feet!"

Maisie — "My husband's got no manners — when he drinks a cup of tea, he holds the cup with his little finger sticking out!"
Mo — "Some people consider that to be good manners!"
Maisie — "Not when the teabag's dangling from it!"

Why did the axe go to the doctor's?
It had a splitting headache!

Why did Mr Dopey somersault down the hill?
He wanted to turn something over in his mind!

Ted — "Why are you dancing with that jam jar?"
Fred — "Because it says on the label 'Twist to open'!"

Mum — "Why can't you amuse yourself for a few minutes, Bobby?"
Bobby — "Because I've heard all my jokes before!"

Have you heard about the dance called the elevator?
It has no steps!

Witch — "I can go into the street and turn a passer-by into a frog!"

Little boy — "I can go into the street and turn into an alley!"

What did one diamond say to the other?
"It's a hard life!"

What did the other diamond say back?
"I think you're brilliant!"

What did one taxi say to the other?
"It's a hired life!"

What did one poet say to the other?
"It's a bard life!"

What did one prisoner say to the other?
"It's a barred life!"

1st comedian — "Your routine should be in a book!"
2nd comedian — "Really?"
1st comedian — "Yes — then I could shut it up!"

Annie — "I wish I were in your shoes!"
Betty — "Why?"
Annie — "Because they're much nicer than mine!"

What does an artist do to relax?
She draws a bath and paints her nails!

Bill — "This looks like a bargain!"
Will — "What?"
Bill — "Violin — two pounds-fifty. No strings attached."

Why did the tailor go to the doctor's?
He had terrible pins and needles!

Politician — "I want my speech to reach thousands of ears!"
Farmer — "Then make it in my cornfield!"

Mother goat, to kid — "Butt me no butts, young man!"

Little boy — "Thank you very much for the dictionary
you gave me, Auntie!"
Auntie — "It's a pleasure!"
Little boy — "Not exactly, but I'm sure it'll come in
useful when I do my homework!"

Annie — "Are you coming to the fire-sale, Betty?"
Betty — "No — I don't need any fires!"

Maisie — "I've been on a chicken diet!"
Mo — "How do you feel?"
Maisie — "Terrible — do you know how little chickens eat?"

Why did Mr Dopey take his dog to the watchmaker?
Because it had ticks!

What did the jumper say to the shirt?
"Want to hang out for a while?"

Maisie — "They say the world's getting smaller every day!"
Mo — "That'll make the postal service a bit quicker, then!"

Little boy — "I'm going to camp this summer!"
Friend — "Do you need a holiday?"
Little boy — "No — my parents do!"

Mum — "Why do you think your teacher is stupid, Sam?"
Sam — "Because she had to ask me how to spell my name!"

Little boy — "Thank you very much for the present, Auntie!"
Auntie — "Don't mention it!"
Little boy — "Okay — it can be a secret, just between you and me!"

Optician — "There now, son; with these glasses you'll be able to read everything!"
Little boy — "Does that mean I don't have to go to school any more?"

Billy — "Were you nervous about being presented with your prize, Jimmy?"
Jimmy — "No — I was calm and collected!"

Bill — "I've just had twelve rides on the carousel!"
Will — "You really do get around, don't you?"

Old man — "I had my first bath when I was sixty five years old!"
Friend — "Why?"
Old man — "Because the best time to have a bath is before retiring!"

Mum — "What are you making all that noise for in the larder, Billy?"
Billy — "I'm fighting off temptation!"

A cyclist was on a country road trying to fix a puncture. Suddenly a horse poked its head over the wall and said; "You'll have to take the wheel nuts off first!" The man was astonished.
Not long after that, the farmer came to feed the horse. The cyclist said to him; "Your horse just spoke to me!"
"What did it say?"
"It told me to take the wheel nuts off — can you believe it!"
"Well," said the farmer, "it knows a lot more about bikes than I do!"

Psychiatrist — "Why are you taking all those biscuits, son?"
Psychiatrist's son — "Oh, they're not for me — they're for my personal demons!"

Little boy to farmhand milking cow — "I don't think the farmer likes you!"
Farmhand — "Why not?"
Little boy — "Because I asked him how to milk a cow and he told me a little jerk does it!"

Mum — "Why can't you go to Lucy's party, Annie?"
Annie — "Because the invitation says from three to six — and I'm seven!"

Fred — "My mother's sister gets great TV reception!"
Ted — "What's her name?"
Fred — "Aunt Enna!"

Why did everybody feel sorry for the demolition worker's children?
They came from a broken home!

Bill — "Our house is really small!"
Will — "Not as small as ours — why, our house is so small that even the mice have round shoulders!"

Maisie — "I feel great on Saturdays and Sundays, but I can hardly get out of bed on Mondays, Tuesdays, Wednesdays, Thursdays or Fridays — why is that?"
Mo — "That's because they're weakdays!"

Why did the man throw the thermometer out of the window?
He wanted to make the temperature drop!

Maisie — "Someone jumped out from an alley at me last night and I fell into a faint!"
Mo — "Very careless of someone to leave the cover off the faint!"

What hand does an ambidextrous chef use to stir the soup?
Neither! He uses a spoon!

Mo — "Your hair looks lifeless today!"
Maisie — "Yes — it's dyed!"

Why did the martial arts expert go to the doctor?
Because he had Kung flu!

When is a hippie invisible?
When he's outta sight, man!

How do you beat the bus home?
Step on some glass, and find a short cut on foot!

Why did the lifeguard have to save the hippie?
Because he was too far out, man!

Why did Batman buy a pound of worms?
They weren't for him — they were for Robin!

What did the big teddy say to the little teddy?
"One more word, and I'll knock the stuffing out of you!"

What did the eggs say when they saw the saucepan?
"Scramble!"

What did one telephone say to the other telephone?
"Who knows what the future might brr-rring!"

Why do cows use vanishing cream?
Because vanishing cream helps the cowhide!

Billy — "I've got something I can give to my friends and still keep myself!"
Bob — "What's that?"
Billy; — "A cold!"

Two burglars broke into a bed shop.
They were caught napping!

There was an archery contest today, but there was no outright winner. The referee said it was a bow tie!

What did the priest say to the sprig of mint?
"Go in peas!"

Why do mothers dress their baby girls in pink and their little boys in blue?
Because babies can't dress themselves!

Why was the Scotsman unhappy?
He had just washed his kilt and couldn't do a fling with it!

What is the difference between Mount Everest and a school dinner?
Mount Everest is hard to get up, and a school dinner is hard to get down!

Bill — "Where's yesterday's paper?"
Betty — "I put it out in the bin!"
Bill — "But there was something in it that I wanted to look at?"
Betty — "Why would you want to look at a pile of potato peelings?"

What is over seventy years old, rides out on the prairie and knits?
The Crone Ranger!

What rides out on the prairie going "bring, bring"?
The phone ranger!

Optician — "Tell me what's written on the chart in front of you, please."
Client — "Are you having trouble with your eyesight too?"

Customer in pet shop — "I'd like to buy this parrot please. Will you send me the bill?"
Pet shop owner — "Not likely! Take the whole parrot, or nothing at all!"

Bill — "It's all over the building!"
Will — "What is?"
Bill — "The roof!"

What do you get if you cross a sheep with a chocolate bar?
A Mars baa-aa!

What did the saucer say to the cup?
"None of your lip!"

Bill — "Why are you crying, Betty?"
Betty — "I baked a special cake just for you, but the dog has eaten it!"
Bill — "Don't worry, he's a tough little thing — he'll soon recover!"

Fred — "I've been playing the piano on and off for years now!"
Ted — "On and off?"
Fred — "Yes — the stool's rather slippy!"

What do American footballers eat their chowder from?
A soup-erbowl!

What do you call a skeleton who rides a horse and wears a mask?
The Bone Ranger!

Teacher — "Where did King John sign the Magna Carta?"
Pupil — "At the bottom, Miss!"

Did you hear the joke about the bed?
It hasn't been made yet!

Did you hear the joke about the very thin insect?
There's not much to it!

Did you hear the joke about the dime?
It's not worth it!

Man (to street singer) — "Do you know your voice drives me mad?"
Singer — "No, but if you hum the first few bars, I'll join in!"

What is the difference between a weightlifter and a sick person?
A weightlifter finds it hard to keep things up, and a sick person finds it hard to keep things down!

Did you hear the joke about the aeroplane?
It'll go over your head!

"My grandma is still alive at 102!"
"That's nothing — my grandpa's still alive at 115!"
"115?"
"Yes! 115 Cherry Tree Avenue!"

Bill — "What do you think of my home-made toffee?"
Will — "Mmmmmmmmmmmm!"

Why did the musician's son take a lump of toffee out to play conkers with?
It was his Nutcracker Sweet!

Did you hear the joke about the birthday present?
You won't get it!

Did you hear the joke about the invisible needle?
You won't see the point!

Did you hear the joke about the guffaw?
It's a laugh!

Did you hear the joke about the dentist?
Aa-aah!

What is the name of the character that appears in every book?
Chap one!

The vicar had a bonfire today.
— **Holy smoke!**

Bill — "Why did you call both your sons Edward?"
Fred — "Because two Eds are better than one!"

Why does superman wear enormous shoes?
Because of his astounding feats!

Criminal — "I was sent to prison for the rest of my life!"
Prison officer — "So?"
Criminal — "You won't let me rest at all!"

"I'm a good speaker — people say I have the gift of the gab!"
"I'm a successful pickpocket — people say I have the gift of the grab!"

Who shopped the bank robbers?
It was the teller!

What do careful criminals do?
Practise safe robbery!

Why are canals burglar-proof?
Because they have so many locks!

What do you call a cannibal who eats his parents?
An orphan!

Barber — "This hair restorer is so good, it makes hair grow on a bowling ball!"
Man — "But that's no good — I want hair on my head!"

Why do flies walk on the walls?
Because if they walked on the floor, they would be stood on!

Why did the elephant wear size ten hiking boots?
Because it had size ten feet!

Annie was visiting her grandmother.
"Would you like to see the cuckoo come out of the cuckoo clock?" her grandmother asked.
"I suppose so," said Susie, "But I'd prefer to see Grandpa come out of the grandfather clock!"

Father — "I took my son to the zoo yesterday!"
Friend — "And did they accept him?"

Lady to paper-boy — "What's your name, my lad?"
Boy — "Bill Clinton, ma'am!"
Lady — "That's a well-known name!"
Boy — "I should think so — I've been delivering the papers around here for over a year now!"

Fred — "Last week my mother-in-law hit me on the back with a frying pan, and she cried for the rest of the day!"
Ted — "With remorse?"
Fred — "No — with disappointment — she was aiming for my head!"

Did you hear about the man who broke into the bank and put £3,000 in the safe?
He was generous to a vault!

The edition published 2008 by
Geddes & Grosset,
David Dale House,
New Lanark, ML11 9DJ, Scotland

© 2008 Geddes & Grosset

ISBN 978 1 84205 672 1

Printed and bound in the UK